EDWARDIAN DEAN

IN COLOUR

VOLUME 1
The postcards issued by Tilley's of Ledbury, circa 1906-1914

Neil Parkhouse and Ian Pope

Lightmoor Press

Introduction

The Forest of Dean is that part of Gloucestershire which lies west of the River Severn and south of the main A40 road from Gloucester to Ross-on-Wye. Hilly, heavily forested and bound on two sides by the rivers Severn and Wye, over the centuries the major transport routes have tended to go round rather than through it. As a consequence, and despite a history of mining and industry that stretches back to Roman times, the communities within the Forest developed and maintained an independence that persists to this day. Only in the later decades of the present century, as tourism has taken over from the traditional industries, which have now largely disappeared, has that fierce independence begun to dissipate.

It was only from the early 1800s that the centre of the Forest really began to open up with the arrival of both the Severn & Wye and the Bullo Pill tramroads. There followed a rapid growth in the developments of collieries, ironworks and tinplate works and consequently, a need for housing the workforce. Most of the older settlements around the edge of the Forest remained unchanged but a whole new town, Cinderford, grew through the Victorian age into maturity during the period covered by the views seen here.

Industrially, the Forest had probably passed its zenith in the late Victorian era. As the nineteenth century came to a close, iron making in Dean came to an end and the last great ironworks in the Forest were closed and quickly demolished, beaten by bigger and better positioned companies using cheaper imported ore. Although coal still had to reach its peak, in terms of tonnage raised, the number of pits in the Forest was shrinking fast as they were amalgamated or exhausted. The future was with the deep mines and, because of increasing mechanisation, not all the colliers who lost their jobs could be found alternative places. The decline though was gradual and hopes were still high of an upturn in fortunes, in a population used to the roller coaster nature of life in an industrial community. It is probable that, in the period covered by the pictures in this book, the realisation of the eventual outcome of that slow, inexorable decline had not yet dawned on the people of the Forest.

The Edwardian era is often characterised as the last great age of innocence, an innocence that ended for ever in the mud and trenches of Flanders. Whilst, as with all such generalisations, there is a deal of truth in this, it is doubtful if the communities of the Forest, used to fighting their daily, weekly and yearly battles with employers, conditions, nature and life itself, could be used to characterise such innocence. Nevertheless, there is an optimism and spirit apparent in many of these views which was certainly not in evidence between the wars. The motor trains on the Great Western's Forest of Dean branch serving the new station at Cinderford, the booming collieries, the busy harbour at Lydney and the proliferation of shops selling all manner of exciting wares that epitomised a country at the height of its industrial success and on top of the world. This was indeed a time of colour, as opposed to the hard, grey world that was left when hostilities finally ceased in 1918.

The northern end of the valley of the Lyd Brook was framed by a graceful viaduct of two 120 foot and one 150 foot spans, towering 90 feet above the valley. Built to the design of George William Keeling, the engineer of the Severn & Wye Railway & Canal Co., by the Crumlin Viaduct Works Co. the line over the viaduct opened for traffic in August 1874. The railway over the top gave an outlet for Forest coal and iron ore to South Wales *via* the Ross & Monmouth Railway. The valley was once heavily industrialised with tinplate works and iron forges and also several corn mills, one of which can be seen here with smoke issuing from the chimney with the mill pond alongside.

Tilley's of Ledbury

In 1869 Luke Tilley, one of five brothers from a Dorchester family, moved to the Herefordshire market town of Ledbury and established a business as a stationer, newsagent, bookseller and printer, in premises on the High Street. Around 1900/01, he started to retail picture postcards of the town. In 1903 one of his sons, John Jacob, trained as a stationer but also a keen photographer, joined the business and opened a photographic studio in an alley behind the shop. From around the same time the great British postcard boom started to happen and it was perhaps inevitable that John would plunge the firm into this market. That he did so with some success, as is borne out by the number of his cards that survive today, says as much about his eye for business as it does about his eye for a photograph and soon there was a growing range of Tilley postcards for sale locally.

It is thought that most of the Forest of Dean, River Severn and lower Wye Valley views published as postcards by Tilley's, were bought from other photographers. The collection of nearly 500 glass negatives, held by Hereford Record Office, only contains a couple of views of the Speech House and the Severn Bridge. Of the pictures featured in these pages, those that have been discovered in photographic (as opposed to printed) form carry the details of other concerns. The view of Lightmoor Colliery, for instance, has been found bearing the initials W. P. (Will Phillips of Gloucester) and also S. & Co. of Cinderford (unknown photographer), although which of these concerns took the original photograph is not clear. It was not unusual, however, for a postcard publisher to buy in negatives to enable coverage of another area to be established quickly and cheaply.

The postcards discovered so far indicate that the northern half of the Forest was rather more extensively covered by Tilley's than the southern. Lydbrook, Ruardean, Drybrook, Mitcheldean, Newnham and especially the Cinderford Valley are well represented in the list. In the southern half, Lydney features strongly but there are only two views each of Blakeney, Coleford and Pillowell, one of Parkend, and nothing of Whitecroft or Bream. Similarly, the Cinderford collieries are well covered but there is nothing on those in the Lydney-Parkend valley. To an extent, this mirrors the list of Will Phillips's photographs, which further strengthens the belief that he was the source of many of Tilley's Forest negatives. Other parts of Dean will feature more in a further volume, which will present cards by other publishers as well.

The influence of the Tilley family on Ledbury was quite considerable. As well as taking portrait photographs of the local people and views of the area, the shop continued to do well and John got involved in other ventures. He was the lessee of all the private poster sites in the town, printing the posters that went on them. Shortly before his death at the early age of 52 in 1926, he established the Tudor House library in premises acquired from his brother William, who had run a motor accessories shop and bicycle hire business in them. William also had a motor garage and car hire business. Tilley's shop and printing business only finally closed in 1988 and Miss Leonie Tilley, John's last surviving sister, died in 1992. Their name, however, lives on, through the postcards and other publications which have survived to become collectors items today.

The Colour Postcards

By and large, the world of our Edwardian ancestors only exists for us today in images that are black and white, be it as photographs or early cine films. This can make it difficult for the mind to visualize that the world they lived in was every bit as colourful as ours. The Forest of Dean, for instance, has always been an area of spectacular beauty, both in the nature of the terrain and the way the seasons paint their character across the landscape. Prior to the invention of colour photography, only artists were able to replicate these colours and convey them down the ages to us. However, for a short period, mainly before the Great War, the twin fields of painting and photography combined to give us an impression of the colours of the Edwardian Age.

The catalyst for this combination was the picture postcard. First permitted in Great Britain in 1894 and therefore a latecomer to the Victorian Age, they captivated the Edwardians who developed and used them to an incredible degree. Between 1900 and 1920 literally billions were issued and bought, creating an incentive to produce ever more attractive designs. Realising colour had a greater sales potential than black and white, some of the more enterprising publishers took to producing coloured view postcards. Many of the larger companies had their cards printed in Germany, where the colour printing techniques were much advanced and considered the best available.

Tilley's had virtually all of their coloured view cards printed in Germany. The most attractive ones were finished with a layer of gelatine, which gave the colours a much more vibrant appearance. Some of them had a matt finish and only two or three colours were used, giving a them a simple 'hand-done' look. It is known that a few of their matt finish cards actually were hand tinted, probably by Mrs. Tilley and although the technique was much less sophisticated and the colouring

very basic, nevertheless there is an insistent charm about these too. Why they should occasionally resort to this method is not clear but, possibly, it was a way of increasing the sales of the black and white views, particularly if they had temporarily sold out of the colour versions. Many of their cards were initially produced in both half-tone and colour.

Surviving examples of photographic proofs sent to the printers by John Tilley are very revealing and contain much interesting information. The instructions were often quite complicated and include requests to add bits into parts of the picture which lacked interest or definition, such as windows in distant houses and smoke curling up from chimneys. In common with many other publishers of the period, Tilley's were also not above pasting people or cars into street scenes, boats into river views and ducks onto ponds to add extra interest. These additions are usually very easy to spot. The colours were generally the photographer's choice and suggested from notes made at the time the picture was taken, although sometimes they were done from pure supposition.

The First World War affected the British postcard trade a great deal. For one thing, for obvious reasons cards were no longer printed in Germany. Tilley's, along with many other publishers, naturally made the most of this in their publicity material, an advertisement of March 1915 trumpeting the 'All British Manufacture' line. It is known that Tilley's were friendly with the well known postcard publishers E. T. W. Dennis of Scarborough (still producing cards today) and there was a distinct similarity in the style of their colour cards. Possibly Dennis's took over the printing of Tilley's cards at this time. Gelatine colored(sic) postcards were advertised by Tilley's to the trade at 6/9d per gross or 6/3d per gross for 7 gross or more.

The Tinting Process

The pictures on these first two pages illustrate well the subtle nature of the colouring process and the different effects that could be achieved. The colliery view, bottom right, relies on the natural buff shade of the card for its base effect, with a rough green tint for the foliage and light blue to simulate the colour of tiles and the sky. The colour has been applied by hand and the back of the original card is blank (albeit with a few paint smudges), indicating that it was a pre-production proof. The Forest view above it, has been coloured by means of a much more sophisticated technique, using different blocks to develop the colours required. Occasionally, the colour would be screened, that is broken into dot form as opposed to a block of solid colour, to give the impression of a different shade. A yellow base was first put down over much of the card, with various blocks of blue and red then being printed on top. In the lighter areas, a single application of the second colour was sufficient, the detail being defined by the black and white half tone background. The darker shades were partly formed by the density of this background and partly by layers of slightly heavier colour. The overall effect of a forest with autumn approaching is very convincing, although the Speech House on the horizon has been inked in.

Close examination of the picture of the Speech House, below, with the aid of a powerful magnifying glass, reveals how this simple colouring process can fool the eye. The whole of the card has first received a very light smattering of pink, almost flesh coloured dots, which served to add tone into areas with no other background, such as the clouds in the sky. The roof, fence and front door have been block-coloured red, parts of the sky in blue, and the grass and the trees green. What looks to be different colours in the grass for instance, and the realistic appearance of the stone walls, have all been achieved by the texture of the black and white half tone background onto which the colour has been applied. The gelatine glaze applied to these latter two views, which added a subtle tint of its own, served to protect the card and to make the colours stand out. The gelatine was applied hot in liquid form to the printed sheets, via ducts in the printing rollers. With age it tends to crack and peel (it is also soluble in water), so the cards have to be handled with care. Whilst there is no way that the shades produced by these tinting techniques can be claimed to be wholly accurate, nevertheless they provide us with a fascinating glimpse of the colour of Dean in the Edwardian Age.

This is the first time that these views have been reproduced in their original colour form since they were published, nearly ninety years ago, and we hope that today's generation are as charmed by them as were the Edwardians.

As the centre of the Forest, both in geographical and political terms, the Speech House has also become its most enduring landmark and, as such, it is the ideal place from which to start our tour round Edwardian Dean. It was originally built to serve two purposes; in 1675 the Forest was divided into six 'walks', each in the charge of a keeper. The Speech House was the lodge for the keeper of 'King's Walk', its construction being completed around 1680. It also housed the Forest Mine Law Court, whose job it was to administer the 'gales' (grants to mine within the Forest) and was the meeting place for the Forest Verderers. The four Verderers, whose job it traditionally was to administer the Forest, continue to meet on occasion today at the Speech House and, spiritually, it is still the home of the few remaining free miners. The original part of the building is the right-hand end in this view, the enlargement being completed in 1861, three years after it had first become a hotel. Note the early motorcycle propped against the fence - the photographer's perhaps?

The venerable gentleman making his way up the Howlerslade valley has just passed the Cannop Foundry of Messrs. Herbert & Young, started in 1835. To the left of the foundry the line along the hillside denotes the route of the Howlerslade tramroad. With the conversion of the Severn & Wye in 1869 to a railway this branch was left to serve the quarries at the head of the valley until 1920.

Waterloo Colliery, probably named after a nearby corn mill of the same name, was first developed in 1841 but proved something of a white elephant until taken over by the Lydney & Crump Meadow Collieries Co. Ltd. in 1908 by which time it formed part of the North-Western United deep gale, formed to develop the deeper coals. After considerable investment the colliery worked until December 1959.

Lydbrook Church.

The Church of Holy Jesus (reputedly the only church in the country with that name) at Lydbrook was completed in 1851 the parish being formed from sections of Drybrook, English Bicknor and Ruardean parishes. Running tight behind the church was the Lydbrook Branch of the Severn & Wye Railway who had to pay the church wardens to keep bushes in the churchyard trimmed to give a clear view of the signals.

Upper Lydbrook and the Peaked Rocks.

The main street looking towards Lower Lydbrook, from the point at which it is joined, on the left, by the steep New Road coming down from the Coleford direction. The wood paling fence marks the start of the approach road to Upper Lydbrook Station and the building behind is Lydbrook Post Office and stores. The railway, supported on a massive stone embankment, runs across the centre of the view.

Ruardean from Shot Hill, looking across the road from Ruardean Woodside in the foreground. The fine Norman tower and porch reputedly dates from 1111, although the rest of the church was rebuilt in the 19th century. Ruardean boasted its own brewery and the Horlick family, of 'Horlick's' fame, originate from here. The excellent tinting process has accurately captured the colour of the Forest stone-built wall.

The summit of Ruardean Hill, at 932 feet above sea level, is the highest point in the Forest. In 1897, to commemorate the Diamond Jubilee of Queen Victoria, a flagstaff was erected here, which served to turn the summit into something of a tourist attraction. This was despite it being a good hour's walk uphill from the nearest station at Upper Lydbrook and with every chance of getting lost on the way!

Forest Church & Harrow Hill nr. Cinderford.

A distant view of the Forest Church on Quarry Hill, taken from Ruardean Hill. The excavations in the centre distance suggest the origin of Quarry Hill's name. On the extreme left is Harrow or Harry Hill, either name is correct, deriving from the earlier name 'Airy Hill'. Beyond the church is the Haywood Inclosure, part of Littledean Walk. The basic colouring of this view would have been Mrs. Tilley's brushwork and executed very quickly.

Ruardean Hill from Harrow Hill.

The Nailbridge to Morse road, built in the late 19th century, climbs from left to right across the centre of this view. The scattered settlement was the result of encroachment by squatters, a widespread practice in the 1800s as the industrialisation of Dean gathered pace. The belief was that if a plot was enclosed and smoke was rising from a hearth by nightfall, the right to build a house was gained.

In the centre of this view stands the newly constructed platform of Nailbridge Halt which opened for passengers in November 1907. The line on which it stands, built by the Mitcheldean Road & Forest of Dean Junction Railway, was never fully opened for traffic. After acquisition by the G.W.R. this portion was opened for mineral traffic in July 1885. In the foreground runs the private Brain's Tramway from Trafalgar Colliery.

Drybrook & "Stenders".

The village of Drybrook nestles at the northern end of the Cinderford Valley and was the northern terminus for the motor trains, the halt just appearing to the left of this view taken from Ruardean Hill. From the Cross, in the centre of the village, the road to the Stenders and the Wilderness leads off top left. The area in the centre of the picture, behind the houses, was known as the Morse Ground.

Drybrook Motor Halt.

The terminus for passenger services on the Forest of Dean branch was a wooden platform at Drybrook with no great pretentions. Services were worked in the main by '2021' Class 0-6-0 saddle tanks with autotrailers which formed the 'Motor Car Service', also known as rail-motors. During the day these trains carried hundreds of colliers to and from work at the collieries around Cinderford. In the distance looms the bulk of Ruardean Hill.

Drybrook & Hazel Hill, from Stenders

After straggling along the road up from Nailbridge, the main part of Drybrook village is tucked tightly into the hills at the end of the valley around the crossroads of the Cinderford to Ross and Mitcheldean to Ruardean roads. The surrounding land was largely agricultural and dotted with farms, heavy industry staying farther down the valley, until the opening of Drybrook Quarry in 1928 and still working today.

The Cross, Drybrook.

The Cross at Drybrook where the Nailbridge to Ross road, passing left to right through this view, formed a junction with the road over the Stenders to Mitcheldean, which is behind the photographer. Heading away from the camera is Golden Valley Road, which led to the rail-motor halt and on to Ruardean. The white painted house in the centre is the premises of Aaron Marfell, plumber and decorator. A number of village children have come out to see the photographer and the two boys flanking the girl in the foreground pose self-consciously for the photographer on a warm summers afternoon. Just visible on the left is the Morse with Ruardean Hill above.

The Hawthorns from Drybrook

The line of the Mitcheldean Road & Forest of Dean Junction Railway to the north of Drybrook Halt was never opened for revenue earning traffic. The railway had been built to provide an outlet to the north for the mineral output of the Forest but was rendered unnecessary when the Severn & Wye Railway & Canal Co. opened their Lydbrook Branch. This view, taken from the top of Drybrook Tunnel immediately to the north of the halt, shows the unused rails curving away past the scattered community of The Hawthorns heading for the northern terminus of the line at Mitcheldean Road Station on the Great Western Railway's Hereford, Ross & Gloucester route. The rails were lifted during the First World War but were reinstated in 1928 when a quarry was started in the fields on the left of this scene. There had been small quarries in the area for many years, together with lime kilns to supply the surrounding agricultural area. Indeed, smoke from one such kiln can be seen rising to the right of the railway. North of Drybrook the landscape changes from woodland to predominantly agriculture on the northern slopes of the Forest.

Mitcheldean. Railway Station & East Dean Hill.

The Hereford, Ross & Gloucester line runs from right to left across the centre of the card with the station at Mitcheldean Road visable beneath East Dean Hill. The H, R & G was opened throughout in 1855 and provided a useful cross country route. To the right of the view lies the village of Lea which was much closer to the station than was Mitcheldean itself which lay some one and a half miles to the south.

Mitcheldean. General View and Cement Works.

The route from the Stenders to Mitcheldean is reputed to be part of a Roman road through the Forest. It curved down into the town past the cement works and, on the left, the Bible Christian chapel. Looking from the spire of St. Michael's church, Tusculum House and gardens feature prominently in the centre of this view. Dr. Searancke lived here for many years.

Mitcheldean, The Cement Works

Opened during 1886 the cement works became a major employer in Mitcheldean. Built by Maynard Willoughby Colchester Wemyss, on whose Wilderness Estate the works was situated, it was initially operated by the Wilderness Portland Cement Co. Taking advantage of the hillside the plant was designed to avoid hoisting materials and for the end product to be at such a height as to be loaded directly onto a wagon. By 1913 some 60 tons of cement a day were being taken to Mitcheldean Road Station and it was reported 'that the transit of the cement works traction engine with its train of trucks long ago reduced the road macadam to a chaos of loose stones, lying hidden underneath some inches of white choking dust'. The works closed in October 1915 due to the break down of the dry mill engine – which was German built and thus the spares situation was impossible! During its life the works had passed through the hands of a number of companies, although the names connected with them often remained the same. At the time of closure the works were in the hands of the British Portland Cement Manufacturers Ltd.

– 14 –

Mitcheldean. (May Hill in the distance)

This colourful general view of the town is dominated by the spire of St. Michael's church, parts of which date from the 15th century. It had been much added to over the years and was substantially rebuilt in the 19th century. In the right background are the premises of The Forest Brewery, owned by Francis Wintle. It was closed in 1923 and fire destroyed part of it in 1926, the rest later being occupied by Rank Xerox.

Old House at Mitcheldean.

At the turn of the century much of the town consisted of buildings of some antiquity, since swept away. These old houses in Mill End were probably at least 200 years old when this picture was taken and, happily, most of them still survive. That on the immediate right had been a pub, The Jovial Collier, until a few years before this view was taken and Mrs. Little's confectionery shop can be seen far left.

– 15 –

Flaxley Abbey.

A Cistercian abbey was founded here in the 12th century by Roger Fitz-Milo whose father, Milo Fitzwalter, Constable of St. Briavels, was supposedly killed at this place in a hunting accident. It was destroyed by fire in the 18th century, being rebuilt in the form seen here in 1777. Henry II granted the abbey many privileges, including free pasturage in the Forest, the right to forge iron and to fish in the Severn.

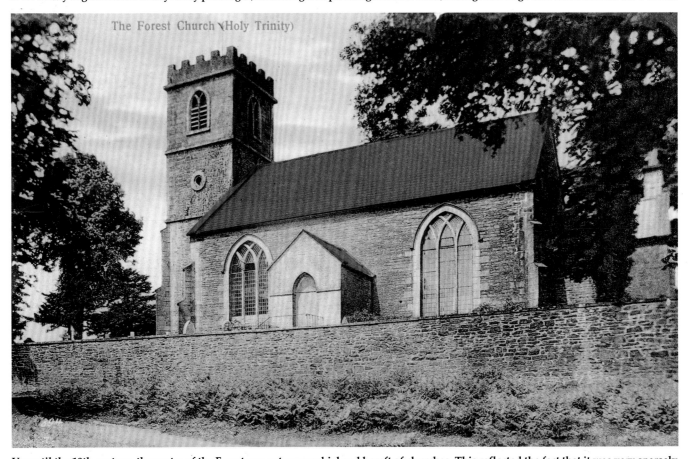

The Forest Church (Holy Trinity)

Up until the 19th century, the centre of the Forest was extra-parochial and bereft of churches. This reflected the fact that it was very sparsely populated and the religious needs for those living within were amply served by the border churches at Mitcheldean, Ruardean and Newland. The growing population led to a need for religious and educational provision and the opening of Holy Trinity in 1817 was a result of this.

Forest Church, Drybrook.

The establishment of Holy Trinity was due to the efforts of the Reverend H. Berkin who was concerned at the lack of suitable premises when preaching to the Forest miners. As the first church within Dean, it came to be referred to as the Forest Church. This pretty view, looking towards Cinderford, also shows the tiny schoolroom built at the same time. Between 1847 and 1866 the Reverend H. G. Nicholls was vicar here, during which time he wrote his three noted books on the history of Dean. At the time, this was a large parish and Nicholls' efforts on behalf of his flock, conducting services at Woodside and the Hawthorns (in schoolrooms he had established), Littledean Hill and Holy Trinity, led to his death at the relatively early age of 44, in 1867.

Steam Mills & Schools nr. Cinderford

Steam Mills school, built in 1882 and with a capacity for 416 children, catered for mixed and infant pupils. Some of its female customers pose a little self-consciously for the photographer, on a warm summer afternoon just before the Great War. The sender of the card refers to the house on the right, in which he used to live, being next to Steam Mills brickworks and comments that the colour of the roofs is wrong!

The main street through Steam Mills with the post office and stores, run by Edgar Bower, on the left. The chimney belongs to the flour mill, established here by 1840 and which, around 1887, was taken over by Wintle's to supplement their maltings at Mitcheldean. Around the same time, the Teague family started a foundry in premises just behind the mill, the business later becoming Teague & Chew.

Cinderford from Coleford Road.

Taken from the Mitcheldean-Monmouth road, this view looks south-east towards the town of Cinderford which straggles across the hillside. The embankment in the foreground once carried a narrow gauge railway in connection with the Hawkwell Colliery, closed in 1896/97. In the middle distance the platform shelter of Whimsey Halt on the Forest of Dean Branch can just be discerned below the trees of Holly Hill Wood.

Foxes Bridge Colliery, nr. Cinderford

Foxes Bridge Colliery lay to the west of Cinderford and worked the upper coal measures for housecoal. Originally sited further south-east, water forced a new start here during the 1860s. In 1908 555 men were employed underground with 86 on the surface. The colliery, at this date owned by the Foxes Bridge Colliery Co. Ltd., worked until mid-1930 when increasing amounts of water and decreasing amounts of coal brought closure.

Trafalgar Colliery nr. Cinderford.

Trafalgar Colliery was actually on two sites, separated by the Serridge ridge, and connected by a narrow gauge railway through a tunnel. This portion of the works went by the wonderfully evocative name of Strip-and-at-it Colliery and was used as an emergency exit and for pumping purposes. In the distance on the right can be seen Brierley, one of the few villages which nestle amongst the Forest proper.

Trafalgar Colliery nr. Cinderford.

The main site, again from the ridge but looking south east. Trafalgar was owned by the Brain family and here in 1882 electricity was used underground for the first time in the world, being generated in the building to the left of the chimney. In 1919 the workings flooded and the colliery was then bought by the Foxes Bridge Colliery Co. and Henry Crawshay & Co. to protect their own collieries from water. Final closure came in 1925.

Crump Meadow Colliery nr. Cinderford

Another of the housecoal collieries to the west of Cinderford was Crump Meadow. Started by Edward Protheroe circa 1829, in 1884 it passed into the hands of the Lydney & Crump Meadow Collieries Co. Ltd. The following year an output of 80,746 tons was achieved. They invested in the work and improved the colliery. In November 1888 they replaced the hemp ropes on the winding engine with wire, being the last colliery in the Forest to do so and in 1890 they installed pumping plant which enabled the practice of drawing the water out of the pit in tanks up the shaft to be discontinued. The early years of the present century saw the colliery beginning to run out of workable coal as a result of which the company acquired Arthur & Edward (Waterloo) Colliery to enable it to continue trading. In 1908 481 men were employed underground with 92 on the surface. Crump Meadow finally closed late in 1929 having run out of economically workable coal and being faced with ever increasing amounts of water to pump. In this view of the colliery the two winding shaft headframes can be seen with the winding engine house between and on the left the Cornish beam pumping engine over the Deep Pit.

The premier housecoal colliery in the Cinderford area was Lightmoor, owned by Henry Crawshay & Co. Ltd. Work started between 1832 and 1835 when Moses Teague was awarded a gale in extension of the Meerbrook Level. He soon interested William Crawshay, a South Wales ironmaster, in the working and Crawshay invested heavily. The pair were also interested in an ironworks at Cinderford and Lightmoor was used to supply the works with coal once it was struck in 1846. In 1854 Henry Crawshay took over his father's interests and a colliery which was

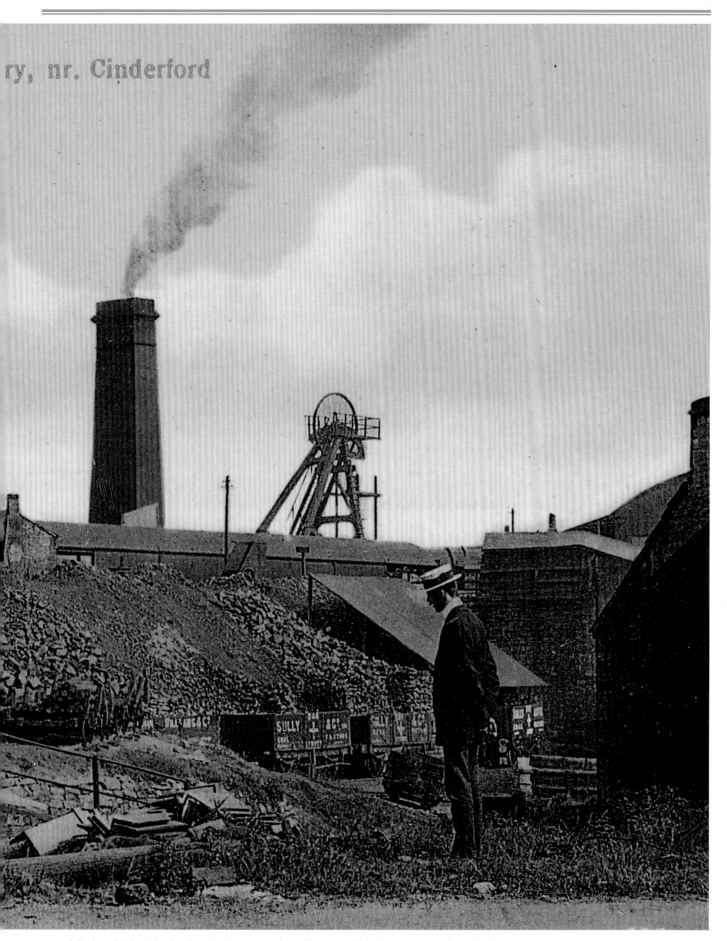

one of the best laid out in the district. Henry ran the colliery until his death in 1879 after which Henry Crawshay & Co. Ltd. was formed and they operated Lightmoor until closure in May 1940. On the left of this scene can be seen the end of the beam belonging to the 78 inch Cornish pumping engine over the Deep Pit which could lift 605 gallons of water per minute. The house which contained the Neath Abbey Ironworks built engine still stands today, a silent memorial to a once thriving colliery. The other two headframes stand over the North and South Shafts.

Cinderford Station from the Railway Hotel

This station at Cinderford was opened on the 2nd July 1900 by the Severn & Wye Joint Committee of the Great Western and Midland Railways to replace the original Severn & Wye station which was about a mile out of town. For many years the inhabitants of Cinderford had been pressing for a more convenient facility and when the Severn & Wye was acquired by the GW & Mid. in 1894 the provision of a new station was written into the Act of Parliament. However, work was not pressed ahead at great speed and caustic comment regularly appeared in the local press right up until the day the station opened. The new station was very much in the Great Western style and gave a neat and efficient appearance. Until 1908 it was used solely by Severn & Wye passenger and goods trains when in that year the G. W. constructed a link to their Forest of Dean Branch at Bilson. After this the Rail-Motor Service began using the station and in this view, taken from Station Street, the rail-motor can be glimpsed through the opening of the goods shed standing out of the way whilst a Severn & Wye passenger train from Lydney arrives at the platform.

– 24 –

Looking south through the station towards the Railway Hotel which can be seen to the right of the goods shed. A Severn & Wye goods train shunts in the yard, having left a van and a Midland Railway brakevan standing on the goods shed road, whilst the signalman leans out of his box window enjoying the sunshine. Above the cattle pens on the left stands a large advertising hoarding, probably owned by E. Roe.

Parish Church (St. John's), Cinderford

Since 1807 colliers had petitioned for the provision of a place for educational and religious purposes in the Cinderford area but it was not until 1842, when the Forest of Dean was divided into four parishes, that a church was provided. The parish church for Cinderford, St. John's, was consecrated on 22nd October 1844. Built of Forest stone to the design of Edward Blore, the incumbent between 1908 and 1927 was the Rev. F. W. Baldwin.

The Triangle, Cinderford.

The road from the station, not surprisingly called Station Street, emerged into the centre of the town after a stiff climb up the hillside just behind the horse and cart. The 'Triangle' was originally occupied by a blacksmith's shop, bought by the townsfolk in 1907 and removed as an eyesore. After the Great War the site was used for the town's war memorial. On the left can be seen Kear & Sons, one of the town's original traders.

High Street, Cinderford

It was once written that Cinderford was 'a network of unlovely dwellings, mostly small, with shops of the co-operative class, where boots and bacon jostle each other side by side'. In this part of town it was certainly true. The red brick shop on the right is the No. 2 Branch of the Cinderford Co-operative Society. Beyond, set back from the road, is the Town Hall, also in the hands of the Co-op whilst on the other side of the road is the No. 4 Branch.

Cinderford, Town Hall and High St.

Looking down the High Street with Ruardean Hill in the distance. The Town Hall on the left was built in 1869 by the East Dean Town & Market Co. Ltd, formed mainly of influential coal owners such as the Crawshays. As a business it soon succumbed and the building was acquired by the Co-op. On the right stands the Lion Hotel 'unpretending at first sight, showing little more than broad bar-window and an entrance door. Behind there are cool panelled rooms, welcome, quick service and tea of a quality that passes praise'. Advertised on the wall between the upstairs windows is the fact that billiards could be played within. At one time Mr. Smith the proprietor of the Lion, ran a horse drawn omnibus to the old Cinderford Severn & Wye Station to collect travellers. Immediately below the Lion is Mundy's hairdressers, denoted by the barbers's pole. The High Street itself was often cause for complaint with its unmade surface of fine furnace ashes and slag dust. In wet weather it was a permanent puddle and in the summer on a windy day everyone benefitted from a dusting of fine black pigment! This was in 1906 and it had only been in 1897 that kerb stones were laid.

Cinderford, from the Railway Station.

The straggling nature of Cinderford is clear in this view with many individual plots originally encroached from the Forest. Built by their owners with no consideration of a communal water supply or sewage provision, problems of epidemic due to water contamination grew until a water supply was provided in 1875. Indeed, in 1869 the town was described as being one of the worst in England regarding layout and sanitary provision.

Cinderford from the Woods.

Looking south-east towards St. John's church on Cinderford Tump the cluster of buildings in the centre were all connected with the Cinderford Ironworks. Here were several rows of back-to-back housing built by the Cinderford Iron Co., a pub and a Methodist Chapel. The waste ground in the foreground was tip space for the ironworks and following closure many thousands of tons of railway ballast were removed from the area.

The Eastern United Colliery, Ruspidge, Forest of Dean

Eastern United Colliery, to the south of Cinderford, was owned by Henry Crawshay & Co. Ltd. It was one of the deep gales formed by the amalgamation of smaller gales after the 1904 Dean Forest (Mines) Act to enable the economic working of the Coleford High Delf seam of steam coal. The coal was won by means of two drifts, or adits, into the hillside - the mouth of one can just be seen to the left of the nearest hut. This view, taken circa 1910 shows early development work at the colliery with the sidings in the course of being laid and no screening plant as yet erected. At this time there was probably little hint of the serious geological problems which were soon to hit the colliery when, due to a fault, the coal disappeared vertically downwards for 150 yards. The bridge over the sidings and the Cinderford - Blakeney road carried waste material to the tip. The GWR's Forest of Dean Branch can be seen above the bridge heading off up the valley towards Cinderford past Staple Edge Halt. The waste tips beyond the colliery mark the site of Staple Edge Quarry, cut into the hillside of Staple Edge, whilst on the opposite side of the railway can be seen the start of the settlement of Ruspidge.

Soudley Tunnel nr. Newnham.

At Soudley the Forest of Dean Branch passed through Bradley Hill by means of a 299 yard tunnel. With a tight bore, a 1 in 48 gradient and on a curve, it was regarded by footplate crews as being more difficult to negotiate than the 1,064 yard Haie Hill tunnel through which trains for Cinderford had to pass before reaching Bradley Hill. On the right is a standard GWR crossing keeper's house built in 1884. The crossing keeper looked after the gates over a lane giving access to some of the more scattered houses that form the village of Soudley. To the left of the railway can be seen a hand pump, probably the drinking water supply for the crossing keeper's cottage as a well-worn path leads across the line to the back door. Several small children can just be discerned in the doorway of the cottage, awaiting no doubt the passage of the approaching rail motor but probably drawn by the novelty of a photographer standing on the bank opposite, ready to capture this view. Behind the cottage there was once a pond fed by the Cinderford Brook, the outfall for which can be seen on the left. It has to be said that at times the stream was less than delightful having been polluted by many industries and by sewage further up the valley.

– 30 –

Newnham, once a busy port and in the 13th century returning its own Member of Parliament, had long since declined in importance. However, the railway station and the ferry, connecting the Forest and the west bank of the Severn with Gloucester and the south east of the county, still ensured the town retained some status. Note the sign pointing to the ferry and the 60 foot high clock tower, erected by public subscription in 1873.

St. Peter's Church, a mixture of Norman, Early English and later styles, was restored in 1875 but destroyed by fire six years later. It was subsequently rebuilt in facsimile at a cost of over £4,000 and the vicarage was built shortly after, in 1888. An impressive Calvary stands in the churchyard, a memorial to the first headmaster of Brightlands school, Mr. Mclaughlin, and his two sons, both killed in the Great War.

Underclife, Newnham-on-Severn

Newnham was built on a small hill, keeping it above the Severn's flood level. There was also a natural shallow crossing point here, later obscured by the river's shifting sands and channels, which led to the fare paying ferry service starting in 1802. The ferryman at the time of the picture, Tom Phillips, lived with his wife and fifteen children in this large house, since demolished due to the threat of river erosion.

River Severn At Newnham.

This rocky promontory is known as The Nab and the ferry service operated from a slipway round the other side. The path in the foreground led from Tom Phillips house. It was here he kept the ferry moored when off duty although it is not the boat featured - the photographer has cunningly cut this boat out of another view and pasted it on to this one to add interest. The ferry service fell out of use after World War II.

The Severn is a powerful and dangerous river, and nothing illustrates this more vividly than the daily Bores which rush upstream. The narrowing channel and the natural downstream flow force the incoming tide into a standing wave, which sweeps up the river and round its many bends, causing a terrific spectacle and sometimes considerable damage. The spring and autumn high tides are the most dramatic.

The Severn Bridge, Nr. Lydney.   (No. 5)

A Great Western Railway freight train can be seen running along the banks of the river, past a fisherman's cottage, on the South Wales main line of the GWR. The South Wales Railway opened as a broad gauge line in 1851 between Gloucester and Chepstow and later between the latter and Pembroke Dock. The train has just passed through the masonry arches of the Severn Bridge which crossed the river by 21 graceful iron spans.

Severn Bridge, West End. (No. 1)

Built between 1872 and 1879 and crossing the river by means of 21 spans having a length of 4,162 yards the Severn Bridge was, at the time, second only to the Tay Bridge and construction was finished before that of the Severn Tunnel. Built by the Severn Bridge Railway, to the design of George William Keeling, the bridge gave access for Forest coal to the deep water port at Sharpness. On completion of the bridge the Severn Bridge Railway amalgamated with the Severn & Wye Railway & Canal Co. to form the Severn & Wye & Severn Bridge Railway Co. A train heading for Sharpness stands in Severn Bridge Station, dominated by the tall signal box which gave a good view across the bridge. The GWR South Wales main line runs through the trees to the right of the masonry arches. Over the years the bridge was struck by numerous vessels drifting up river on the tide in fog or bad weather but thankfully little damage was done until a fateful night in 1960 when two petrol barges collided in fog and, drifting into the bridge, brought down two of the small spans. Despite years of debate the bridge was never repaired.

– 34 –

Blakeney Hill was another area settled by squatters, who also claimed common or pasture rights for their animals. In 1831, a Commission set up to inquire into the Forest was forced to recognise the squatters position and give them their deeds. The issue of the common rights went unresolved, as it does to this day, but the passage of time has given them much substance and the sheep continue to roam at will.

A view of Blakeney from the bridge that carried the Forest of Dean Central Railway over the High Street. This line had failed even before it was completed and by this date saw only an occasional lightly loaded goods train. Blackpool Brook, in the foreground, joins Bideford Brook just beyond the farther bridge. Children from the Public Elementary School, built in 1873, are enjoying their mid-morning break.

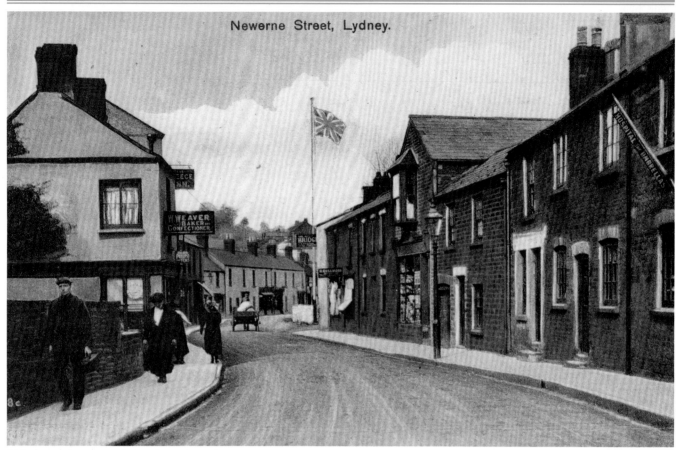

Newerne Street, Lydney.

Lydney grew as a port, being the main outlet for Forest coal. After the conversion of the Severn and Wye tramroad in 1868, it became an important railway town too. There was a monthly cattle market and three annual fairs, including a wool and stock fair in June. This view shows Weaver's bakery and the Fleece Inn on the left and the Bridge Inn, Gulliford's jewellers and the Umbrella Hospital on the right.

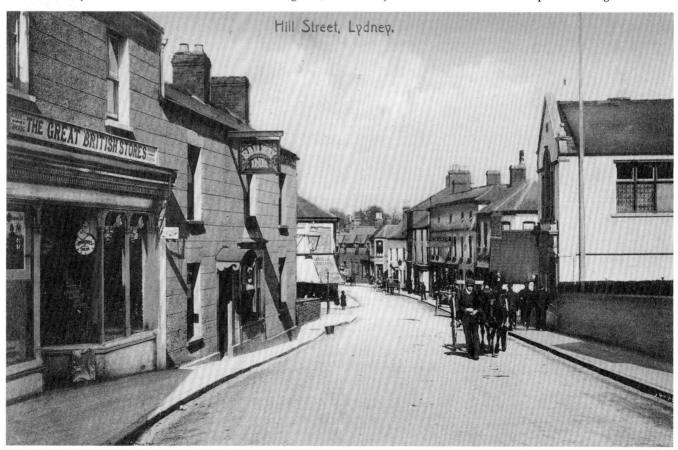

Hill Street, Lydney.

Hill Street looking north from the railway crossing; Newerne Street started the other side of the junction with Whitecroft Road, on the corner of which can be seen Gosling's outfitters. Gilbert Gosling was also the proprietor of the Alexandra Hall. Lydney Picture House, built in 1913, was situated just past the Railway Inn and *The Lydney Observer* was published from offices in Hill Street every Friday.

Railway Crossing, Lydney.

Taken from further up Hill Street and still looking north this view shows the level crossing of the Severn & Wye Railway. By this date the S & W was owned jointly by the Great Western and the Midland Railways and it was the Great Western who supplied the brick-built signal box, the rear of which can be seen to the right of the crossing, in 1897. At the same time improvements were made to the crossing, which was now controlled by a wheel within the signal box, to save the gates having to be opened by hand. The crossing was always regarded as something of a nuisance both to local commerce and to through traffic and in 1902 it was pointed out that the Severn & Wye Joint Comittee were obliged to carry any public road over or under the railway by means of a bridge. How that could be accomplished here is unclear but as a result the footbridge was provided in 1904 at a cost of £567 – which is what the locals really wanted! The horse and trap turning into Hill Street beyond the level crossing has come from Arnold Perrett's brewery stores. Again, the photographer has captured people's interest including the street cleaner with his wheelbarrow; the reason for his presence can be seen alongside the barrow!

– 37 –

The Docks, Lydney. (No. 2)

The harbour and canal at Lydney, built by the Seven & Wye Railway & Canal Co., were opened in 1813. This view shows the Upper Basin at the Lydney end of the mile long canal with a ketch being loaded with coal at one of nine such tips. The tip is of the original square type which, from 1897, were replaced by tips with a single upright, seen behind, the advantage being they needed less men to operate them. Railway coal wagons with opening end doors ran onto the tips by gravity and were lifted on a platform to enable the coal to slide out through the end door, down the shute, into the vessels hold. On the right of the view is a rake of Parkend Deep Navigation Collieries Co. Ltd. wagons, standing on the Upper Docks branch, which have brought coal down from one of the company's collieries to be loaded at the company's own tip. The majority of coal shipped from Lydney went to the West Country, especially Bridgwater, or to Southern Ireland. The buildings to the left of the rake of wagons were the original offices of the S & W R & C Co. which at this date were occupied as stores and offices by William Jones, a builders merchant who also owned several vessels trading out of Lydney, notably the *Black Dwarf*.

Lydney Docks. (No. 1)

From the Upper Basin a canal led down to the Outer Basin and the River Severn. Something of the activity which took place at Lydney is apparent here with a number of vessels awaiting loading. Some are Severn Trows, used on the river alone, whilst others are ketches used in the West Country trade. Many vessels trading into Lydney came from Appledore in north Devon and numerous links were fostered between the two communities.

Lydney Church

The spire of the Church of St. Mary at Lydney had been rebuilt barely a decade before this picture, a gale having blown it down in 1896. St. Mary's could trace its history back some 700 years to the Early English period. The chantry at the end of the north aisle, at one time the private chapel of the Bathurst family, had a memorial window installed to commemorate the men of Lydney who fell in the Great War.

Lydney. The Cross & High Street.

Lydney saw much bitter fighting between Parliamentarians and Royalists in the Civil War, during which (circa 1644) St. Mary's church was burnt to the ground and the 14th century cross was dismantled. It was restored in 1878 by the family of the late Reverend W. Bathurst. On the far side of the cross, construction of the Capital and Counties Bank is just starting, on the site of a recently demolished house.

The Forest of Dean (near Lydney).

This delightfully rural view, taken on the Lydney to Whitecroft road, shows piles of stones on the left for use in repairing the surface, when required. The timber wagon appears to be collecting birch, possibly for tying into besoms (brooms with lime wood handles). If so, this makes this view rather unusual; the 'underwood' in Dean was little worked compared to other forests and few pictures were taken.

Pillowell nr Lydney.

The slopes rising eastward from the village of Whitecroft were also colonised by squatters, evident again in the scattered nature of the housing, eventually forming the communities of Pillowell and Yorkley, the three villages straggling one into the other as they climb up the hill. Note the drift entrance on the right and the children out to watch and pose for the photographer - still a great novelty!

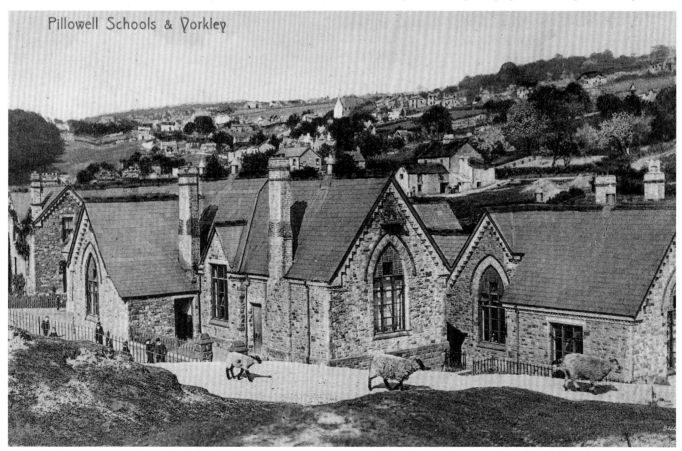

Pillowell Schools & Yorkley

Pillowell Public Elementary schools were built in 1878 and included a residence for the headmaster, visible on the extreme left. Also serving Parkend, Whitecroft and Yorkley, they were enlarged to cater for 500 children in 1898. In the centre distance, the Baptist chapel of 1860 stands out above Yorkley village. Some of the areas ovine inhabitants are flaunting their common rights in front of the camera!

Parkend.

Parkend was once a thriving industrial centre with a blast furnace, a tinplate works, stone works and several collieries. By this date only Parkend Colliery survived, part of which can be seen on the hillside directly above Parkend House. The house was occupied by the colliery's owner Thomas Hedges Deakin. As a result of the industrial activity the railway provision at Parkend was extensive. In this view the 'New Road' into the Forest, built by the Crown in 1905, passes through in the middle foreground and is crossed by the railway heading towards some loading sidings in 'The Marsh'. The timber-built goods shed and station buildings are products from the Gloucester Wagon Co. to a design by William Eassie. The importance of Parkend can be measured by the fact that it was provided with two platforms and a footbridge. The signal box on the left was provided by the GWR in 1897 and controlled the level crossing for the Coleford-Blakeney road. As at Cinderford the desolate area of ground in the foreground is the result of tipping ashes and slag from the ironworks and here too, many thousands of tons were removed for ballast and road making purposes.

– 42 –

Coleford, Church Tower & Station Road.

Until the rapid 19th century industrialisation of Dean, Coleford was the largest town, the only market and head of a petty sessional division in the Forest. In 1894 it was constituted as a civil parish and an Urban District Council was formed to administer the town. There was a monthly cattle market and fairs in June and August for the sale of wool, cattle and cheese, all held under a market charter granted in 1661 by Charles II. This view of Market Place, from St. John's Street, shows the remains of the octagonal church of St. John, built in 1821 and demolished in 1882, being replaced by a new church of the same name a little way to the west and in a more elevated position. The town centre also housed a Town Hall, built in 1662, and just to the left of this view. Behind the church tower is Station Road which gave access to both a Severn & Wye station and a Great Western one. The Severn & Wye route led down to Lydney via Parkend whilst the Great Western took travellers down to Monmouth and thence to Chepstow, Ross or South Wales. Soon after this view was taken the latter line closed in December 1916.

SPEECH HOUSE HOTEL. FOREST OF DEAN.   268c

A final glimpse of the Speech House through the trees ends this colourful meander round Edwardian Dean. Visitors to the Hotel at this time faced a stiff 20 minute walk uphill from Speech House Road station, unless they managed to connect with the occasional motor charabanc service that ran through the Forest in the summer months. They were also advised to instruct the stationmaster at Lydney to telegraph ahead and order lunch, which would be prepared in time for their arrival. This agreeable way of seeing the Forest and visiting the Speech House came to an end when passenger trains ceased to run north of Lydney in 1929 and from then on the motor car (and the drive-in picnic site) gradually took over.

An advertisement for Tilley's products which was printed on the back of a stock postcard. The thought of being able to purchase 100 cards for the sum of 1/3 (7p) would send modern day postcard collectors rushing for their time machines! The period prior to the First World War was certainly one of different values in many ways.

Photographed and Published by Tilley and Son, Ledbury

POST CARD.
TILLEY'S SERIES

AFFIX STAMP

Printed Abroad

FOR COMMUNICATION THIS SPACE MAY BE USED.

THE ADDRESS ONLY TO BE WRITTEN HERE.

Transfer of Business.

Great VALUATION SALE.

50,000 Post Cards of your District

Collotype, as this.   All Clean and Fresh.

Offered at 1/6 Per 100   (Assorted), Cash with Order.

1/3 This offer only holds good during the Sale.

See list enclosed for Views of your District.   May we send an assortment ?

TILLEY & SON, Post Card Publishers, LEDBURY

Acknowledgements and Credits
Grateful thanks should firstly go to Dennis Parkhouse, without whose considerable support this book would not have been published. Much assistance has also been received from Alec Pope, whose knowledge of the Forest of Dean and its people is extensive and freely shared. David Postle has given us full access to his large collection of postcards and paperwork relating to Tilley's of Ledbury. He also kindly supplied information on the Tilley family plus certain details regarding the processes used in printing the cards and his contribution has been invaluable to the finished book. David Smith has likewise been most generous in allowing us access to his collection of Tilley postcards. We need to thank Ian Standing, curator of the Dean Heritage Museum at Camp Mill, Soudley, for allowing us to use some of the cards in their important collection. Finally, we must record our appreciation to the folks at Artytype for their professionalism, enthusiasm and friendly assistance and to Clare for her proof reading.

Pictures (the numerals are the page numbers, 'T' refers to the top illustration on the page and 'B' to the bottom)
David Postle Collection   : 2, 4, 6B, 9T, 10T, 12, 14, 20T, 20B, 24, 26B, 30, 32B, 40T.
David Smith Collection   : 5T, 5B, 6T, 7T, 7B, 8T, 9B, 13T, 13B, 15B, 16B, 17T, 18T, 25B, 28B, 31B, 33B, 34, 35B, 36B, 37, 41B, 42, 43.
Dean Heritage Museum   : 8B, 10B, 11, 18B, 19B, 26T, 29, 35T, 36T, 39B.
Pope/Parkhouse Archive   : 15T, 16T, 19T, 21, 22/23, 25T, 27, 28T, 31T, 32T, 33T, 38, 39T, 40B, 41T, 44.